Waiting To Say Amen

Waiting To Say Amen

By

R. S. Carlson

ISBN 978-0-557-48978-7

DEDICATION

To my wife, Ruth,
who loves and sustains;
to our children, who keep me young;
and in memory of my Mom, Dad and Aunt Mamie,
who embodied prayerful service to others.

ACKNOWLEDGEMENTS

Poems have appeared in literary journals as follows:

Arcturus:	Baptism; Speeds of Light; Forms
Bitterroot:	Jerusalem Stone
Cube:	A Chair in the Sun
Grapevine:	Veni, Emmanuel
Hudson Valley Echoes:	Seams
Medicinal Purposes Literary Review:	Hummer
Peck Road Magazine:	Eucharist
Pilgrim Review:	Of Gatherings; Of Martyring; Of Cloistering
Poetry/LA:	Night warps; Second Story Finitudes
Poets On: Loss:	Diagnosis
Porcupine Literary Arts Magazine:	Iglesia de los Angeles
Praesidium:	Devotion; Diagnosis II; Diagnosis III; Diagnosis IV; Hike
Protea Poetry Journal:	Dream
Sculpture Gardens Review:	Grasp
Studia Mystica:	Madonna; Of Pilgrimage
The Cape Rock:	Creche; Elements; Thinking I Could Learn to Love Her; Waiting to Say Amen
The West Wind:	Coast; Tones, Hues, Saturations, Lights....; When I Am Gone
The Panhandler:	The "A" Ward

CONTENTS

Tones, Hues, Saturations, Lights...

I write to disappear... to make others look at the world more closely....

Shirley Graham

At surface, the soft voice synapsed
almost too quickly into our neurons
artist, titles, the hues of fruit in the shade,
the swans bent elsewhere,
the distant figure departing.

So when we meet the color print
in the art book on someone's coffee table,
we will seem to recall it was
in San Francisco we saw the original, --
or was it Chicago?

How many times past pennies in the cash drawer
can breath seize us by the larynx
for more than polite applause?

Forgetting the first cause
for this seeming *deja vu*
came through an almost-whisper
"I write to disappear,"

We will wait as if
    bowled fruit scrolled vision
    riper than light
    or swans winged off the water
    into three dimensions,
    and the departing figure on the cobblestones
    glanced back to wave
when we turn the page.

Jerusalem Stone
(On hearing from the travelers)

The myrtle cube penholder on my desk
shows me Jerusalem's skyline
in relief on a copper medallion.

Another traveling friend left behind
the Hebrew-English prayer book
bound in silver.

For all the stills and footage
I have seen of cobbled streets,
spires, minarets, markets, shrines,

troops on patrol, bombed buses,
mourners irate over coffins,
prayers at the Wailing Wall,

until tomorrow permits my feet
pilgrimage among thousands wearing
cobblestones and shrine sills concave

with Abrahamic quests,
I count, by your ear,
the chink of masons' chisels,

and warm, through your eyes,
in sunrise brazing
those walls of Jerusalem stone.

Madonna

From the black mound of shawl and skirt
the copper face and hand
point into the flow of passers-by.

Draped half in the mother's lap,
half on the pavement,
the infant sleeps.

The toddler, three steps off,
turns toward the glimmer of foil
fallen into the gutter scrap.

The mother's hand catches the toddler's wrist;
he strains toward the brightness
beyond the fluttering of feet

as the mother's hand aims his
back at the passing faces,
forcing the palm upright.

Iglesia de los Angeles
(Colonia El Tecolote)

Behind the lock,
the churchyard is fenced dust.

Three weathered two-by-six crosses
lean into the neighbor's wisteria,
awaiting next Easter's procession.

Behind the padlocked doors
wait the folding chairs,
the hangered vestments.

The walls, boarded warm with evening,
allow three pairs of windows
to blink their quarter panes --
    here cracked, there broken --
into the sun and dusk.

Inside, framed print stations of the cross
stagger between
the dusty permissions of light.

Behind the altar hangs a banner:
"Gracias Dios por venir con nosotros."

Who keeps the key?
Where is the Padre?

Of Gatherings
(To the Female Prophet)

Holy Mother,
Ave.
Care for your canon:
it enthralls.

You say you only testify?
True,
but you are remembered -- worded -- beatified:
the saying is the sainting;
the said, the sanctified.
Look to your canon:
it enthralls.

    Forgive my dribbling
your sweet wine in my beard;
and if my beard is unforgivable,
forgive, at least, my wish to sip --
though uninitiate --
that kind of your eucharist.

Take me for a doddering Samuel, now,
-- first a gift of the sexless to the barren,
returned as first fruit to the shrine
to be acolyte to old Eli:

-- childly upright,
an innocent who heard a voice in the night
in a shrine,
and had to be told
not to answer to a man;

-- an altarboy
who had the rules by rote,
and tattled to the greyed Pater
of the priest-sons'
extorting the best offerings at the doorway,
and taking the loveliest women
in the pillared court;

-- a small prophet
given unwieldy word of death;

-- a boy, devout and fearful,
compelled to answer to a patriarch --
fat, devout and failing --
who knew a voice had spoken;

-- then, when doom fell true,
successor to prophet role
for tribes familiar with hollow texts
and tunes of priestly corruption;
tribes which cried to be a kingdom
till a voice
gave a name,
and I poured holy oil on a head,

then watched the young king
snatch at power, and prophecy, and priesthood --
early, searching for voice,
then steadily deafening
until
I heard the voice,
poured oil on a shepherd's head
and waited.

So much for me, Holy Mother.
Look to your canon.

Ours, you know, is much memorized:
so yours will be:

many mouths taste of something more than text
and less than truth;

when a mouthful is all that can be managed,
the metaphor conveying truth
becomes the truth itself;

the life struggling to be born
at the womb's mouth of language
takes an image:
> the image iconifies to letters;
> the word ritualizes to law;

so, to the inescapable icon
come scribes to schematize,
artisans to adorn
till brilliant breath stands immured
with scrolleries of convention.

What are you now in first passion?
Does your gathering tell a whole joy?
> Ours tells for today and for always,
> though many look to the telling
> with one eye or the other closed;
> ours tells impartial love for the partial,
> though many ignore the paradox,
> and we tend to hawk tickets
> for orchestra, box and loge
> at invitational performances
> of a polished tear
> or a comfortable custom.

Who are your chosen people?
   We have two strains entwined:
   the born and the broken.
   Among them, of course, orders and clans
   convene, combine, contend
   and divide,
   taking exception to one another's exclusions --

   for a suppliant does not always know to present,
   nor a healer always know to bind
   the greater wound;
   nor the singer know her own deafness,
   nor the silk seller see his torn hem;

   sister and brother cannot always hear
   their names lilted in old dialect;
   and the same anthem,
   mother-clear at the altar,
   echoes oddly
   down the aisles of cathedraling time.

Does your tribe in-gather the outcast?
   Cherish the gathering warmth,
   and hone cautiously
   the blade of young convert zeal;
   the cutting edge of tear-tempered righteousness
   guts and quarters blood sacrifice swiftly;
   I count many scars
   on my slowing hands.

Does your creed declare an evil?
   Some looking into our scriptures
   find an incarnate devil
   generating all wrong;
   I find this devil
   consistently steals mirrors;

some see sin as infertility --
life worst profaned
in the barren mind,
the fruitless soul.

Does your community celebrate a eucharist
of one kind?
    Well, what does that matter,
    if you know why?
    Passion is as well celebrated
    in the spilled as in the broken.

Ave, Holy Mother.
Care for your canon.
Can you nurture your joy to resist
too quick a catechism?

How your wine sparkles now.
Can your stronger novices see
    the grape is not the vine,
    the vat is not the press,
    nor the decanter the aging cask,
    nor the sparkling wine the full communion?
    However devoutly engraved the silver cup,
    the drink too long in the chalice
    only slakes the thirst
    of a hand's breadth of the vineyard path.

Can the converts trim the icons
and still attend the voice?

Ave, Holy Mother --
may we meet again as feast days allow?
Perhaps
come winter?

Of Martyring

Ave, Holy Mother.
Peace be with you in your pilgrimage.
No, I have no questions now.

Yes, when litanies read
in strange dialects,

when vestments are hung
in different hues,

when creeds proclaim
the poles of a paradox,

the true believers will
inevitably kill --
mud for the miter,
and a miter for the mud;

find a plan of God,
and define a God of Plan.

How steadily we move
from ecstasy to altar,
from altar to walled shrine,
from walling in to walling out:

from deliverance
to defence,
to destruction.

Still, live utterly, Holy Mother,
live all your deity provides;
for, of all we would embrace in our travels,
many we can never touch;

some we must let grow away,
for we -- and they --
are already walled up in flesh;

and of the faithful we hold close,
struggling for voice --
those we do not stab
we may smother.

Of Cloistering

Ave, Holy Mother.
Do you suppose we could ever escape
our old competing cloisters?
Our competition is easily proved
by a stroll through the marketplace.

Dress me as a brother in your habit,
your apparent chaplain,
and we shall hear from public lips
how fair, how true

and literally divine
are the maxims
and the distortions
of your confession:

how lethal, how pernicious
the myths of mine.

Dress you as a sister
in traditional orders
to walk with me,
and we shall hear
how fair and true
and literally divine
are the maxims

and the distortions
of our confession:
how blasphemous, how lethal
the tenets yours tenders.

What resort is there
when new insight has grown to new order?
When new heartcry has roused
an increasingly tonedeaf chorus?
When the native thrill of collective chant
has drowned the sense of the words?

Could we escape to search again
for the voice we heard start these earthbound echoes?

Do you suppose, Holy Mother,
you and I could escape
our comfortable cloisters:
set aside the matriarchal wimple
the patriarchal cap;

fold our clichés
over the backs of our gilt sanctuary chairs;
hang our biases
on brass pegs in the vestibules;

cut away the roles and customs
(so long ago sewn to our skins for penance)
to drop beneath the roses by the garden path
while we,
bleeding and naked,
clamber over the garden walls
and bolt unnoticed
for the wild wood --

possibly to cross each other's trails,
possibly to meet in new-scarred nakedness,
possibly drawn together
by the common search for the heart of the wood
where we once walked with the voice
in cool evening?

Somehow, Holy Mother,
I fear we have
still too many festivals to bless;
still too many confessions yet to hear;
still too many processions through the town to lead;
still too many pious retreats behind
still too many cloister walls
still too high for climbing.

Yet there are times when, for me,
the persona wears through to the person;
the vestments lose luster in the dusk;
the hair shirt itches in the night,
and, as I turn on my cot,
breaks loose from the stitching.

Then, up with the pale moon
after midnight prayers,
I stand at my small cell window
and face the wild wood,
listening,
listening . . .

and though the valley between
is wide and dark,
I sometimes think I can make out
the walls of your cloister,
and the outline of your cell window
where, it seems,

a shadow stands,
facing the wild wood,

listening,
listening,
too . . . .

Of Pilgrimage

Now, Pilgrim,
wish the Holy Mother well,
and follow the mountain trail --
still seized by the mystery.

On the far hills,
the Holy Mothers, the Holy Fathers
gather their faithful
to festivals in the cloister churches.

There the icons shine,
never dim with candle smoke;
plaster eyes weep;
brass hands move in blessing;
believers are confirmed in ecstasy.

Why did you disturb the priest
polishing icons at midnight
in his sleep?
Why didn't you give thanks
for the sponge and tube
behind Madonna's head?
Why did you cut the threads that ran
from the patron saint's arm
to the treadle under the altar?

The cloisters on the far ridgeline
glow with torchlight.
At this distance,
the festivals have no voice.

Here in the wood,
naked flesh meets the wind,
vested only with scars
where old stitching torn open
heals over.

Here the incense of earth and air
rises in evening rain.
Wind chants among the leaves.

Clouds in purple
shift to break a brief wafer of light
over the mountain.

Lips taste of sweat.

The eye watches the path
dissolve in dusk.

Ahead,
through the syllables of wind
rising in high trees,
the ear catches
a settling of wings.

Second Story Finitudes
(Hands. Ears. Eyes.)

Hands accustomed to
    locking doors, to
        clasping promises,
    visions in prayers become the
givens of canon. . .

Ears open less for
    accents of a
        tongue known entombed than
    leathered knuckles pounding
against a barred door. . .

Needing, but still not
    ready for, flash
        strobed on retinas
    limp to waves beyond
what spectra we see,

eyes narrow as though
    aimed at fine print
        in dim light, tuned for
    adjusting to far more than
just the present dark.

Devotion

Abuela, in her good black lace rebozo
this Easter morning, steps her four-foot-eight
sixty-nine years over the threshold
of Iglesia de San Francisco.
She wears all black.
She is a modest woman of the faith
in this world filled with pains and devils.

This is the feast of the Resurrection
of the Virgin's Son. The sanctuary
is crowded beyond anything her cataracts
blurred from her before.
The padres she can hear chanting mass
at the high altar, forward.
She must venerate the Blessed Virgin.

One side pew past the entrance
waits the Holy Mother of God,
larger-than-life-size plaster, jeweled,
robed blue and white under garlands of roses.
Abuela genuflects, reciting her "aves"
across the seven teeth remaining
to bless her daily tortillas.

"Amen," and Abuela lifts herself
to find the next open seat
or the next station for meditation and prayer.
But suddenly she sees the padres
have done it again. Not only the faithful
fill the pews, but norteamericanos, too,
have come, -- dozens of them -- to sing.

Abuela twists her scarf tight to her cheek.
She turns up the side aisle.
The seats are jammed on the main floor, and
even the side pews have gringos in them.
Just before the next saint's niche,
Abuela turns to the side pew again.
Where is there rest for a faithful woman?

Here, where there should be respect
for Abuela's grey hair, for Abuela's old bones
weary with diligence, the chantry pulls all eyes
to Monsignor at the altar. Where she longs to sit,
the space is filled -- father, mother, and young son --
by paste-skinned devils on this, the feast of the
Resurrection of the Son of the Virgin.

For all this, Abuela must pray.
The decades, the stations demand it.
Let the young world go on with its mass.
There are saints yet efficacious
niched even nearer the high altar.
And for this bleached-wheat-flour family, too,
a word whistles through her seven teeth: "Coyotes!"

Baptism

The new parents carry
    forward their sleeping pink
        infant. The minister

invites other children
    down front to watch, and they
        flutter forth, surrounding

all -- parents, godparents,
    minister. We in the
        pews and choir page to the

order of service to
    begin, urged to recall
        what word and water were

and are for each of us,
    wet to a death and a
        resurrection. While we

hear the first charge to the
    parents, a young couple --
        center-left aisle, walks out.

Beside their vacant space,
    Grandfather keeps his chin
        granite; Grandmother daubs

the water from red eyes.
    The young wife stops in the
        foyer and turns against

the wall, her husband's hands
    pleading at her shoulders.
        They move on to dry air.

In sanctuary, we
    chorus the creed. The child
        keeps peace with the wet rite

in glad arms. Syllables
    flow through us, last used here
        by most of us, but last

used by two next to an
    incubator, mixed with
        waters broken too soon,

waters almost too scant
    for cruciform, words gone
        too blurred for the child's name.

Eucharist

Kneeling, we take the wafer and the wine,
knowing and not knowing the very ghost
who broods our blood-red ferment from the vine.

The cruciform in wood or brass design
marks all tradition ever gained or lost.
Kneeling, we take the wafer and the wine.

Our fingers on the chalice down the line
show skin's twists from birth to dust.
Who broods our blood-red ferment from the vine?

An infant turns toward blessing, held supine
in mother's arms, firm in mother's trust.
Mother takes the wafer and the wine.

Leaning toward the rail, nearly nine
decades into the puzzles of growth and cost,
an elder sips the ferment of the vine.

Teen and father, solo parent, the sine
waves of flesh and hunger tuned and crossed,
kneeling, we take the wafer and the wine --
our brooding, blood-red ferment from the vine.

Creche

Noon. December twenty-
fourth. The Methodist church
lawn still squares the cyclone

fence around the wooden
hut and manger used for
seven nights' living creche.

The tape deck and speakers
sit mute in the office
beside the Jesus doll.

One Wise Man idles in
traffic, presuming the
freeway will move faster.

The other two are home
vacuuming and taking
out the trash before guests

arrive. Two shepherds will
return at five for choir
practice. One is cruising

Maxwell Street looking to
score an off-white Christmas.
Mary's calendar says

no, not this month either.
Joseph gases up the
Bronco at Texaco,

punches the trip meter
back to zero to mark
mileage from some was to

might be. At the creche, the
donkey crowds the fence. Three
sheep huddle in cold rain.

Speeds of Light

No, if the moon did
turn to blood, day would be simpler:

some last trumpet blare
would rouse rumored powers into

the open to line
up survivors for the last choice --

glee or screech. Whether
registered by eon or by

nanosecond, it
would, at the least, the last, conclude.

For now, before sun
drops, the moon rounds, anemic, through

acid clouds edging
respectable blue evening.

The eye tears to the
airs that eat so slowly we

only half know our
cancers will thrive to outdo us.

But that half of fact
that recurs, spurs, cuts. It restarts

bleeding, and spasms
that close the eye even to this

defective daylight.
Heat marches glazed, pulls muscles taut

till curse, or nurture,
or simple sweat all dry to rime

turned grit for the next
time the hand grasps the steering wheel,

and lane lines blanche in
another glass shout of the sun.

Wrong Man, Wrong Words

1 - A

The hospital hall is too
short. The visiting hours are
almost over. I should turn
around and forget the whole

thing. The man was my mentor
two years back. How can I say
this? I owe him nothing, or,
if anything, undisturbed

rest. When he sees me, he will
spread that grey mustache to his
sneer for us mental midgets
just beginning to think some

serious thoughts in his field.
I am not his rabbi, -- just
some former 'modest promise.'
He will scorn me like whale's breath.

2 - (Alpha)

The intuition is all
wrong. He is agnostic to
his home tradition. He sees
me still too tolerant of

literalists, and his wife
greets me with my name rephrased
to a form featured in old
gullible-husband farces.

Were I the earnest, prepared,
Bible-bearing tract-passer,
I would have the lines polished,
certitudes to force a choice.

This tumor hangs too vague to
be orthodox... His door... Chat
blurs... "Three days I've felt compelled
to come and say 'God loves you.'"

3 - (Aleph)

*No, don't go... Help me over
to the bathroom. The nurses
won't be back for two more hours...
Damn! The morphine only half*

*helps. You know I'm not devout.
No, help me to the wheel chair...
In fact, I've only prayed three
times in my life ... First in the*

*trench in Italy when I
almost lost the leg, bleeding
all night... Second when we thought
our son had drowned in the Rhine,*

*and -- let me grip your hand... it's
still two hours to the next shot...
when they found the kidney big
as a football -- this was Third.*

Thinking I Could Learn to Love Her

Arms of water reach inland. Forest
crouches downhill to the bay's edge
to see itself. Wind leaves a few
leeward mirrors for Douglas Fir posing
with swatches of sky, but teases
open channel to lizard skin twitching
everything there is to see to crumpled-
foil reflections, from foothill
solemnity to the stuttered peeps of
freeway headlights through dusk at
the S-curve across the bay.

I stare, wanting to see God walk out
of Tomorrow with Forget-Me-Nots riding
the third button of her blouse -- the
top two being open for breeze to cool
her borrowed body -- a small chest of
dubloons and crusadoes under one arm just
so I can endow an orphanage across the
border and not worry about retirement, and
a bottle of well-fruited cabernet in her
other hand for us to celebrate
this particular epiphany.

A Chair in the Sun

Sometimes the day forgets what Mother says.
The sun won't stay in place. It loses light.
The children run away without their names.

Sometimes her husband leads her where she goes.
She pushes her chair further into sunlight.
Sometimes the day forgets what Mother says.

A man she doesn't know calls her the same
sweetheart names her husband does tonight.
The children run away without their names.

They never feed her here. The doctor knows
and doesn't help, but puts her pills in chocolate.
Sometimes the day forgets what Mother says.

Her daughter talks too fast, like TV shows
the grandkids watch. Have we eaten yet?
The children run away without their names.

Sometimes her ears need better batteries,
but otherwise everything is right.
Sometimes the day forgets what Mother says.
The children run away without their names.

Elements

Poppies face the sun and genuflect.
Winds twitch dandelion, rose and oak.
In rain, the spans of root and seed connect.

Footpaths crease the field. Mice collect
seed beneath the orbit of the hawk.
Poppies face the sun and genuflect.

The storm that brittle branches would expect
to serve a thirst may flash a killing stroke.
In rain, the spans of root and seed connect.

The light that draws new stems to stand erect
may sweat the leaves to shrivel from the stalk.
Poppies face the sun and genuflect.

Water swells the seed, and we project
a harvest -- till the fields swim and soak.
In rain, the spans of root and seed connect.

Furrowed seasons till us to respect
the best our hands can spade from fields we walk.
Poppies face the sun and genuflect.
In rain, the spans of root and seed connect.

Grasp

Two-hours-twenty-five-minutes freeway
time and we have Dad back to vigil after
an overnight away with us. We park
behind the nursing wing. We will take

his bags to the apartment later. The halls
shine. Here a poster, there a painting
colors the corridor. The floor tiles glow.
Some room door name plates carry photos.

Turn, turn, and Mom has a sweet-smiling
white-haired room-mate this week. She does
not speak. Last week, Mom fell. Now, a
waist strap keeps Mom in a wheel chair.

Hi Mom. We're back. The room-mate turns to
watch. Right elbow on the chair arm, Mom
leans her cheek on her fist. Her eyelids
droop. Hi Mom. We're back. The room-mate

watches, smiling. Across the hall a woman
bawls HELP ME. HELP ME. TODAY. NOW. NOT
TOMORROW. TODAY. HELP ME. TODAY. HELP ME.
NOT TOMORROW. TODAY. HELP ME. NOW. NOW.

We touch Mom's onion-white arm. Are you tired?
No. Are you hungry? No. Has dinner come yet?
No. See the present we have for you? No. We
put the gift -- a cup -- in her hands. She tries

to drink. No. I don't want it. No. Take it.
We stroke her arms. She reaches for Dad's hand,
for mine. Do you remember me? No. Yes. No.
I don't know. I don't want it. Okay. Okay. Mom

shuffles her feet as if to walk. The chair is too
high. The aide is supposed to come on toilet
schedule. The tray is supposed to come on meal
schedule. Aunt Mary will use the knife, the fork,

the spoon. She will remind Mom to chew. The
sedative, the insulin will come on medication
schedule. Dad and Aunt Mary will take their
turns tonight, tomorrow, day after tomorrow...

We take Dad back to the apartment for sandwiches,
then slip back to see Mom. The light is out. Mom
is asleep. Her room-mate smiles and watches. Across
the hall, someone has been helped to sleep.

The soiled linen carts are sealed. Someone watches
TV. Another Alzheimer's patient glides past us in
the hallway. We will come back. We will talk with
Dad. We will talk with Aunt Mary. We will take the

two-hours-twenty-five-minutes freeway time one way and
the room-mate will watch and smile and the woman across
the hall will bawl HELP ME. TODAY. NOT TOMORROW.
TODAY. HELP ME. And we will hold Mom's hand,

and she will say No. Okay. No. And we will
talk with Dad. And we will talk with Aunt Mary.
And the floor tiles will gleam. And Mom will shuffle
her feet, strapped to her chair. And we will be no help.

The "A" Ward

We get to Mom's room
ten minutes before shift change.
This time, the diaper is still fresh,
and no one has slipped her
the bedtime medications
before the dinner tray arrives,

so she can still recognize
we are stroking her hand, greeting her,
and she can still force a grin,
"Ok, ok, ok, OK, OK, OK, OK!"
that ends in a great grimace
showing her lower denture is out.

We have brought back the engagement ring.
Last visit, we saw the band was broken,
and we worked it over her knuckles,
upsetting her. Dad opens the tissue slowly,
holds the new-polished gold-and-diamond
close for Mom to see.

"Look what Dad has for you," I say.
Mom grabs Dad's wrist, pulls his hand
forward, aiming the ring for her mouth.
"Oh, oh," we say. "It's not for eating.
It's your ring. You remember, don't you?
Let him put it on your finger again."

We work the ring back over her knuckle.
Mom grins to grimace stage once again.
This she seems to understand.
We persuade her to seat her lower dentures.
We give her water in her new thermos.
It will be harder to chew apart than the old cup.

Our themes in the room counterpoint
the Reverend Jason at the end of the hall.
    "OH DEAR GOD ALMIGHTY, PLEASE SEND
    SOMEONE
    TO OPEN THIS DOOR FOR ME!"
    "OH DEAR GOD ALMIGHTY, PLEASE SEND
    SOMEONE
    TO OPEN THIS DOOR FOR ME!"

Dad borrows a marking pen from the nurses station.
He writes Mom's name on the thermos cap,
the thermos bottom, the thermos cup.
    "OH DEAR GOD ALMIGHTY, PLEASE SEND
    SOMEONE
    TO OPEN THIS DOOR FOR ME!"
An aide heads for the end of the hall.

The aide tells the reverend,
"You can't go out, now. It's raining today."
It is time for shift change. The aide wheels
the reverend into his room and closes the door.
    "NO, NO, NO, NO, NO, NO, NO...."
Usually, he sings "I'm Forever Blowing Bubbles."

I go to the water fountain to refill Mom's thermos.
Swing shift is signing in, taking report.
The Reverend Jason is wheeling back to the locked exit.
    "OH DEAR GOD ALMIGHTY, PLEASE SEND
    SOMEONE
    TO OPEN THIS DOOR FOR ME!"
The charge nurse wheels him back to his room.

Through her straw, Mom sips the little thermos dry
in two minutes. I stroke her hand. I tell her
about the old photos we have found -- Mom in Duluth,
Mom in San Francisco, me -- at three months --
barebottomed, on a blanket. We laugh together.
We seem, almost, to connect.

"OH DEAR GOD ALMIGHTY, PLEASE SEND SOMEONE
  TO OPEN THIS DOOR FOR ME!"
The Reverend Jason is back at the locked exit.
Sister Cora Blaine, who usually paces the halls
in curious peace, has had her fill.
"Oh, Shut up! Open the door, my rear end!"

  "OH DEAR GOD ALMIGHTY, PLEASE SEND SOMEONE
  TO OPEN THIS DOOR FOR ME!"
  "OH DEAR GOD ALMIGHTY, PLEASE SEND SOMEONE
  TO OPEN THIS DOOR FOR ME!"
The charge nurse wheels him to the nurses station.
"Now just relax. You'll be very sleepy soon."

The freeway traffic will be thickening.
Dad will feed Mom when the tray comes.
Mom grins goodbye, straining against our lips
as we kiss her forehead. This time,
she does not pinch or bite.
Dad hugs us goodbye.

Two aides wheel the Reverend Jason to his room.
  "NO, NO, NO, NO, NO, NO, NO...."
They hoist him from chair to bed.
  "GOD DAMN YOU ALL TO HELL FOREVER FOR THIS!"
  "GOD DAMN YOU ALL TO HELL FOREVER FOR THIS!"
  "GOD DAMN YOU ALL TO HELL FOREVER FOR THIS!"

"Goodbye, Mom." "Goodbye, Dad."
"Lots of love. We'll be down again, soon."
The Reverend Jason, behind closed doors, still mourns:
  "GOD DAMN YOU ALL TO HELL FOREVER FOR THIS!"

Sister Cora Blaine steps past us in curious peace.
We head for the car. For us, some doors still open.

Waiting to Say Amen

The hallway to mother's room breathes
wax. Its handrails, beveled for fingers
seeking grip on something firm whether
birch or not, brace pastel walls that

hold in the oxygen tanks, the railed
beds, the wheel chairs, the linen carts,
the visions short as detergent ads in
afternoon TV, long as the memories splicing

across the joints of two centuries. The
eyes see so much less, now. The hand
clasps so little, now, and so
seldom, but remembers -- almost -- to

clutch, and holds the questions up to
our lips, -- the whethers, the whens of
today's breath, tomorrow's sleep or
day-after-tomorrow's waking. We

shuffle the risks of guilt, waiting
again as we used to wait, heads bowed
above the kitchen tables that served
up the countless family devotions, the

serial prayers in the near-dozen
parsonages where we children peeked at
each other through partly-folded fingers
telling God our specific blames and

blessings in turn, wondering -- while the
out-loud recitations grew longer -- if
Jesus would really come tomorrow like Mr.

Palmer, stamping snow off his boots on the
front porch, hooting steam into winter

air with his greetings. To squirm, then,
impatient under holy things we could only
half know, played us two ways guilty at

least, half glad that Jesus was
listening, but wondering when he would
reply, and how, -- since he hadn't sent
any letters recently -- although Mom and

Dad could tell when he answered, and
kept us trim to chapter and verse so
we could hear the answers, too. But
the itch to tease, to poke the

sibling sitting with eyes piously
still closed; the itch to run out
to play in the back yard thrashed
us to doubt that Jesus would

still be listening when the prayers
grew warm and long en route to the
common chantry of the closing. We sat
uncertain, then, at kitchen tables.

We sit uncertain, now, at the bedside,
speaking as though the unspeakable were
not happening, as though guilt did not
ply us for pricing both a life and a peace.

We speak as though we were not every
day listening for words that made sense;
as though we were not waiting for the
knock on the door that called prayers'

end; as though we were not still
children peeking through our fingers,
waiting to run madly out of here,
waiting to say 'amen.'

Forms

The pink forms
glare up from their clipboards
the too-obvious sketches of breast –
frontal, right and left.

The thin woman
with grey-blonde curls
Puts her purse over her clipboard.
She picks up her self-help happiness book.

Reading happiness,
she need not look at
the strange man beside her,
or the yet-to-be-marked charts on her lap.

The lab staff
Always take too long
To call too soon
For those fifteen steps to X-Ray

She has already paced
a thousand times
during the night
that refused sleep.

Night warps

under parallels that
knot in the glow
of stars

that swallow their own light.
E cubes M and
half C

by times without equals,
parentheses,
or points.

What number of things, un-
real, negative,
zero

distances which always
dwarf love red, blue
and void

while dry hands clasp fingers,
and neutrinos
cross hearts?

Diagnosis

1) Have a seat, please. And please
try to relax. Having some nodules
or lumps in the breast tissue is

normal and, at certain times in
your cycle, they will commonly be
more prominent than other times. We

will watch them, of course, and do keep
on with your self-examination as usual.
Arrange your next visit at the front desk.

2) Hello again. Now you really shouldn't
worry too much. Yes, a couple of these lumps
do seem more distinct on the film this time, so

let's have you come back for another couple
views. They do seem a bit larger to the
touch as well. Do you have a history of

cysts or fibroids -- as far as you
know -- among the women in your family?
Arrange your next visit at the front desk.

3) Well, I'm afraid the mammograms show
enough of something that we should go in
and take a look. What we probably will
find in there are a few cranky little
cysts to get rid of. It won't take
very long, really, and you don't have

to plan for much time away from work or
school. The procedures go quickly these days.
Arrange your next visit at the front desk.

4) Please have a seat. I'm sorry to have
to tell you the biopsy reports came back
positive for malignancy. Unfortunately, the

cells in the lumps are of a type that usually
starts somewhere other than the breast, so
we really need to do further tests to see

what may be going on somewhere else that
brought the problem to where we found it.
Arrange your next visit at the front desk.

5) Please have a seat. The bone scan and
CAT scan came back to us clean, as far as
we can tell, and the blood work should

be back to us soon. Unfortunately, the lab
has had a couple people out sick, and the
reports are coming slowly this week. We

expect to have those results for you very
soon, however. Please try not to worry.
Arrange your next visit at the front desk.

6) Have a seat, please. You can relax.
The last of the tests are in, and they
show no signs of malignancy anywhere

else in your system, even though that
cell type we found very rarely arises
in the breast tissue first. But now,

we already know it's out, -- it's
gone, and it was only breast cancer.
Arrange your next visit at the front desk.

Hike

On the trail from the
canyon rim down to the crash
and spray of river,

daughter scrambles two
switchbacks ahead, leaping rocks
at speed that Mother --

were she here to watch --
would find cardiac arrest.
Father calls, but his

"Careful!" and "Slow down!"
wander into canyon zags
and elbows, sandwiched

between rim road wheel
whines and water arguing
tango or conga.

Canyon air currents
braid themselves broad enough
to lure human ears

to seeming silence
compressed between two streams
of mechanic speech.

The older boot takes
gravel more soberly than
young sandals anxious

to wade shallows, -- froth
at the ankles, crawling shins --
till the skin shakes blue.

The mid-life hand finds
ledges bevelled for slow grasp;
the teen fist skips rocks,

overdone wafers,
across blue-green turbulence --
all for action's sake.

Can the mixed quartzite
flutter all the way to shore
opposite? Let fly!
Would the next grey shale
outcrop serve diving board if
river slowed to lake?

She sings to herself
in the river noise. He sees
the arms, the mouth move,

sees river throating
itself channel, grain by ton,
by million-acre-

feet-per-minute: stone
versus flow: unlikenesses
opposed at her toes;

sand to stay, and sand
to browse downstream; soil parted
by stones, for sage roots. . . .

From a dry ledge just
above the canyon floor, he
waves. She sees his mouth

moving. He sees hers
move, too, before she turns to
wade her next shallows.

He wonders who walked
these ledges last century,
last millennium.

He wonders what she
sings among the river's ten
thousand contraltos.

He waits with boots on.
He watches his child turn stones.
He watches sunlight

stalk shadows while both
crawl canyon strata down steps
too thin for sparrows
or cliff swallows, where river,
stone, child wear one another.

Diagnosis II

2.1) Have a seat, please. Let's
take a look at the lump you say has
appeared on the arm. Since the

breast lumps were not good, we
certainly do need to watch any new
developments closely. Don't

worry yourself unduly. Every day we make
new advances in taking care of these things.
Arrange your next visit at the front desk.

2.2) Please have a seat. The biopsy
on this latest growth also shows a
malignancy. We've scheduled you

for admission to the hospital for
chemotherapy. You should sign in
at Admissions this afternoon if at

all possible. The agents we now use work
better, and give fewer unpleasant side effects.
You may call your family from the front desk.

2.3) How are you feeling now? How is the
room service in this hotel? Is the food
any good? Since this problem cropped up,

we have gone back over the CAT scan pictures,
and we do think there are some abnormal
densities on the uterus and ovaries. We

want to see how they respond to this chemo, but
we may have to consider taking them out. When
the nausea passes, sign yourself out at the desk.

2.4) Please have a seat. The last set of
pictures still show several questionable
areas on the uterus and ovaries. The chemo

does seem to have reduced them somewhat, but
frankly, we should have seen dramatically better
response. We now see surgical removal as the

one safe option, and we feel getting those
affected organs out as soon as possible is best.
You may call your family from the front desk.

2.5) Waking up? You are doing well. We
think we got all that bad tissue out, now, and
the surrounding structures all seemed healthy

when we finished the job. We'll schedule
another regimen of chemo to go after anything
that might be too small to see. Let the nurses

know if you need something for pain. When you
are a little more awake, Recovery Room people will
see you get back to your own room and your visitors.

2.6) Please have a seat. I trust you are
feeling well. The incision looks very
good and, if the tenderness is decreasing as

you say, then everything should be back to
normal for you soon. Here's a prescription for
hormones. We'll adjust dosage as needed. Let's
start the chemo regimen next week. Call
if you notice anything at all unusual.
Arrange your next visit at the front desk.

Dream

Charging, flying, it staggers
us through the dark,

clutches inside the breastbone,
then twists -- laughing at

how we pull at air -- and the
muscles trained for sucking in

wrench against themselves,
gaining nothing, and in our eyes

or, from some false feed like the
optic nerve, scenes crash upon

what we thought we knew: the ceiling
flies off; the stairs fall away

from our feet; footsteps out of light
track closer and closer till a

hand grabs, a dog whines for
leftovers at the aunt's picnic table

in -- where was it now? -- or next year,
who was driving the boat? Who was

on the water skis until the rocks
and the bridge . . . the pistol . . . ?

. . . the sharp edge of
breath breaks open finally in

high sweat: the faces we
wake to smile as if they

had not stalked us, raging,
through so much sleep . . . .

Diagnosis III

3.1 Please have a seat. Let's put
these films up on the light so we
can see what's going on with you.

This last checkup shows us two
new spots on the lung and several
more in the liver and right kidney.

We'll go after these with another
good regimen of the chemotherapy.
Arrange your next visit at the front desk.

3.2 Have a seat, please. That's a
cute kerchief you have there. The latest
films show we are gaining on those

spots in the lungs, but the ones in
the liver and kidney seem to be just
about the same, so we'll try a little

different recipe in the chemo for the
next few sessions. Keep that smile, now.
Arrange your next visit at the front desk.

3.3 Please have a seat. Let's get
the films up again where you can see
them. Here is the old view of the

right lung, and here is this week's
view. Looks like those bad guys are
gone, now, see? That's one for us, and

two to go, right? We'll change the
mix on the chemo again for the next series.

Arrange your next visit at the front desk.

3.4 Have a seat please. We seem to have
some stubborn spots, still, in the liver
and kidney. This set of films shows them

all slightly reduced, but still hanging
on. We'll keep the chemo at the same
mix this time, but we'll also add some

radiation treatments to your regimen. I
trust they won't disrupt your schedule.
Arrange your next visit at the front desk.

3.5 Please have a seat. The current
films just arrived this morning. As you
can see here, the bad spots on the

kidney seem to have given up, so we
just have those in the liver left to
chase with another round of chemo and

radiation. Got a new kerchief, didn't you?
Yes, these sessions are a real drag, I know.
Arrange your next visit at the front desk.

3.6 Have a seat please. Let's get all
these films on the light for you. Here. The
befores and the afters. See?

Clear. Clear. Clear here, too. Start
planning your next hair style. Make sure you
get enough rest. Be sure you stick to a

balanced diet, now, and let's have a checkup
again in six months. Happy Nineteenth Birthday!
Arrange your next visit at the front desk.

Coast

Turn off the engine.
Wait till the
surfer van slams shut
and vibrates
down stereo road,
then open
the doors to the breeze.

Gulls cruising
onshore winds alight
on trash cans,
or waddle the sand,
patrolling
for edibles dropped
by humans.

Out on the rumpled
lame' of
the bay, the otters
slide, licorice
strips bobbing between
uncertain
sequins, waves that pull
the eye to
sunlight, first for joy,
then for glint
too harsh to watch as
a seascape.

Lie back, eyes shut to
blearing light.

The young waves shove and
giggle past
the rocks for the sand:
such schoolgirl
catechumens dressed
white to kneel
then turn back again,
whispering
beneath the chantry
of the shore...
the shore...the shore...the
shore...the shore....

Diagnosis IV

4.1) Please have a seat. Yes, the follow-up films
look clear, still. No, Dr. Jones won't be seeing you.
He's been reassigned. Yes, we realize he suggested
a bone marrow transplant, but the board disagrees.
Please arrange for your next visit at the front desk.

4.2) Have a seat, please. Yes, your attorney has contacted
the review board on the transplant issue. However, your
tests are clear now. Furthermore, the rare type of
malignancy you presented has never responded to transplant.
Please arrange for your next visit at the front desk.

4.3) Please take a seat. Let's look at these latest scans.
We've noted these ambiguous features in the brain before.
Head injury when you were six years old, wasn't it, and
a little residual scarring still showing? We'll watch it, too.
Please arrange for your next visit at the front desk.

4.4) Have a seat please. Everything on these films looks the
same. The blood tests are fine. You should be feeling good.
The little shadows on the brain haven't changed a bit. Still
nothing but that residual scarring we saw. No bad spots.
Please arrange for your next visit at the front desk.

4.5) Please have a seat. Again the scans show nothing new.
And you have no new symptoms to report, right? Since the
Cedars
of Hope consult your attorney arranged concurs your type has
never responded to auto-transplant, it would be purely
experimental.
Please arrange for your next visit at the front desk.

4.6) Have a seat, please. Again, the reports look good.
As long as you feel so well, why put more stress on the system?
Yes, your attorney is dealing with the board. If arbitration
goes your way, we'll refer you to University Hospital.
Please arrange for your next visit at the front desk.

4.7) Please have a seat. It's been a couple months, hasn't it?
How was it at University? The post-transplant isolation can be
tough, I'm sure. Flu-like symptoms? No way to spend your
holidays.
Seen psych, yet? Relax! We can do another set of scans and tests.
Please arrange for your next visit at the front desk.

4.8) Have a seat, please. From these scans, it looks like
we'd better go back to chemo again. That cranial tissue has more
shadowing this time. Spots show again in the lungs, the right
kidney, the liver, the pancreas. First chemo, then cobalt.
Please arrange for your next visit at the front desk.

4.9) Please have a seat. When you take her home, see that the
IV's are changed every four hours. Give the morphine every two
to four hours as needed. I'd say get a hospital bed into the
apartment if you can. Your contract allows two weeks hospice
care.
Ask for Discharge Planning at the front desk.

4.10) Back again? Is Demerol any better than the morphine?
We need to keep these IV's going if you can't hold your lunch.
This is a busy place. If they won't answer the call bell,
then just do it in the bed. They'll change the sheets eventually.
See you again on the next rounds.

4.11) Sorry, but we really need the bed space. You'll just have
to take your questions up with Discharge Planning and your
attorney.
I'm sorry, but these latter stages are unpredictable. It could be
three weeks or three months. The chance of remission is nil.
Now please, take your other questions to the front desk.

4.12) Look. I didn't negotiate the contract -- your employer's
broker did. Hospice care is available for the final two weeks of
the terminal illness. I can't involve myself in home care issues.
My duties are here in the wards and the clinics. I can't say when.
Go back and ask for Discharge Planning at the front desk.

4.13) ... age twenty ...beloved daughter of... sister of...
graduate of Mountain High School, attended Crest College, active
in
Girl Scouts, Amnesty International, Save The Whales... requested
no religious observance... cremation, ashes scattered at sea...
memorial gifts to Family Cancer Fund, Box 7344, Crest City....

Gusting

... to fifteen miles per hour, the
wind abrades a horizonful of sea, and
where sunlight travels,

the water reports itself silver,
blue, green, and wrinkled -- except
in kelp beds held brown and smooth.

White caps flare a moment then
fall back into the rumpled sea more
often, more widely than two eyes

carry account. Again we have
come to the edges of things: the
gulls' white soaring that takes the

eye so easily it fills the wharfside
art shops in pastels and plasters; the
kelp bulbs loose from the sea bed. Again

we listen -- even as we turn away --
to wave wash on the rocks, conversation
we almost understand, keeping answers

embedded somewhere to those questions we
might, could we catch our own breath in this
wind, still somehow lure into words.

Waiting with the Body

As we had done intermittently
in the last three days
when spooning ice chips
into her dry mouth,

I stroked her forehead,
stroked her cheek,
stroked the wrist and hand
that lay above the sheet.

We had been doing vigil --
Dad, a couple of us grown children and wives
driven or flown away from work
with a couple of our children, too, to round the bedside --

not really intending
neoclassical perspectives in
who stood where when
or who posed how to pray,

but waiting for the implications
of the last three years to
unfold themselves from the
staggered signs.

The phone call at midweek
had attuned us for the last of it,
and we convened those who could and would
from the third and second generations

to sit with her and Dad,
and to take Dad out for the haircut,
for groceries, or for Sunday dinner
just to be away from it all for an hour or two,

but always taking the corridor back to
the room where it was happening, and yet was not,
while the pulse swooped to forty, to normal, to
imperceptible to eighty to sixty two,

and the breaths chugged ragged
and harsh for hours, and we spooned in
a little more crushed ice to wet her tongue,
and she sometimes choked and sometimes swallowed

immediately
as though she had asked us for the spoonful,
and we wondered what was happening,
and she rolled her eyes as though she really saw

the one of us holding her hand,
or stroking her forehead,
and then her breathing
stopped

for fifteen, twenty seconds
and we tensed,
stopped
chatting among ourselves and then

she
gave a long sigh
and the breathing
resumed quietly.

Nurse taking vital signs shifted from hourly to
fifteen minute intervals, but it grew late and Dad was tired,
so he kissed her and said "Good night, Sweetheart.
I'll see you in the morning," and went back to the apartment.

The rest of us resumed turns holding her hand,
stroking her forehead,
or sponging her brow with a damp cloth for whatever
comfort it might have been in the low fever,

talking and waiting,
deciding to leave ourselves,
then staying a little longer
when the quiet breathing

went to the
rough and short rasps
again for a stint,
and her eyes again roamed, half lidded,
side-to-side,

and we never
got quite away from
surprise that her skin
was so tight to the bone,
slightly mother-of-pearl
under the fluorescents in the room
and that, with her dentures out,
her lips pulled inward and pursed as though
she was mocking us with a parrot's beak
in one of those old stories she used to tell children
in days before she ever imagined

we
would be allowed
into a room
to see her like this;

and then her head
that we every-so-often arranged
for her in one spot or another
on the pillow

pulled decidedly to center,
and she opened her eyes wide and looked
straight up at my wife -- who at that moment
was holding her hand and stroking her brow --

then closed her lips
in a dignified profile and
let the last breath
go.

The women all cried out softly and leaned toward her.
Big Brother went for Nurse who checked the vitals,
now absent, and asked the time for the records.
Nephew ran to bring Dad back.

Nurse arranged head and hands
and ran the bed flat, saying morticians
sometimes got angry if the body
bent into awkward positions.

I assured her that,
given pending cremation,
the esthetics of repose were not
our first concern.

Nurse left to phone report to the attending physician.
Even though it was late,
Big Brother left to phone down the list of relatives,
administrators and clergy who needed soonest to know,

Our younger daughter left to cry a while.
Dad and nephew returned from the apartment.
Brother, the daughters-in-law and granddaughter came in with
them.
We all joined hands for a prayer, then started the good-byes.
The women left
on the businesses of grief, and
Big Brother resumed
phoning down the list of need-to-know.

Dad took the chair on her right, and clasped her right hand
I stood at her left, stroking her hand,
stroking her brow, sometimes
talking to Dad

as he and I
stared at her stillness, still, but still warm
and looking that commonplace of
'more asleep than when she slept alive,'

Dad and I
attempting to learn
the calm of surprise
in the long/short hour

until
Nurse came in again and said
the man was here.
It was time

    to meet in the corridor
    the polite man
    with respectful dark suit and black tie
    and soft-spoken assurances that

    everything
    was arranged as per contract and we
    had his sincere condolences on her loss as we
    left him to his cover sheet and his gurney,

but before we pulled the drape to leave,
we each kissed Mom good-bye.

Seams

Our customary landscapes we
expect to show us just our own routines.
Leave it to the archaeologist
to plan when and where to dig below
the surfaces we walk or dance or sleep on.
Who cares what yesterday can show tomorrow?
But chance insists it has a bone to pick
with any life gone smug for long.

One time it is someone digging peat,
another time, someone digging coal,
or a whole crew excavating below
the foundation of some late-century building
to ground a newer, more massive glass-eyed
hive, or someone making museum pieces
out of more of Herculaneum,
or someone cross-country skiing along
ice faces pared by an overnight
dry wind, and suddenly, the body,
the skeleton is there.

A few beads,
perhaps, sometimes a dagger, a ceremonial
garment code the find. Once in a while,
the leather tatters of stomach admit of a last
meal before cataclysm -- intended
or otherwise -- left the remains pressed
for time. Commonly sited without language,
the bones offer only the syllables
of wear, the seams of breaks healed, often
awry, always sealed with surplus calcium.

The chewer of sinew wore teeth to the gum.
The swordsman, the spearman, bred muscle to bone
superbly, the cartilage rooting deep collars,
the more active joints clearly enlarged.
The horseman bowed his femurs. The clubfoot
begged, hard put to thicken his ribs.
The pelvis that bore most men and most
children curves most open under
the millenia, and the infants,
in sacrificial jars below the hearths,
no longer buried, but classed, named, and numbered
by what seams of soil chance cut open,
huddle still, messages for the gods.

When I Am Gone

When I am gone,
    let me go.
            If there must be
a picture on a wall,
    let it be one with
            daylight on green leaves
around me.
    If there must be boxes
            and papers by the drawerful,
sort them down
    to a few albums
            someone actually wants

for dreaming back through
    the mountains, muds,
            rains, winds and snows I once walked,

and maybe a poem or two
    someone will actually
            wish to read again.

I could fall ugly
    and slowly fade,
            memory gapping
half centuries to and fro.

        Take the photographs
            from helpless days, and

the circular letters plainting
    shreds of stories I once knew
            to the fireplace for farewell.

By the year I am gone,
>> Lord knows what fool words
>>> I will have fired or misspent,
> or how much I may have hurt you.

>> But I urge you to drop the dross
>>> from what images of me remain to you.

I may not deserve, by then,
>> the least of your mercy –
>>> but you do.

Veni, Emmanuel

Surprising
how well washed

we come, blood
on our hands,

to take the
cake bodied

before us
into small

pieces and
eaten by

light of the
trick candle

we never
really

can blow all
the way out

Hummer

Slim, curved, the black
carpet needle beak

stitched at the overhead
web stretched yellow in

the light left fifteen
minutes before sunset,

and the thumb-sized green
body glowed still iridescent

in the dusk between jacaranda
and pine, holding moments

before a pearl of pine sap
tipping a twig, then

flitting to a miniature
fly bound to the almost

invisible . . . then
gone.

   And we step
again into the growing

dusk, entrusted with a
glimpse of worship.

CPSIA information can be obtained at www.ICGtesting.com
Printed in the USA
LVOW06s0142150814

399254LV00001BA/152/P